Revolting Records

by

Anne Rooney

Illustrated by Mike Phillips

Check out:

www.annerooney.co.uk

www.facebook.com/AnneRooney.author

First published in 2012 in Great Britain by
Barrington Stoke Ltd
18 Walker St, Edinburgh, EH3 7LP

www.barringtonstoke.co.uk

ISBN: 978-1-78112-071-2

Printed in China by Leo

Contents

Get Ready for the Records!

Which smells worse, rotten meat or human sick?

Which would be nastier to eat, smelly fish or smoked bat?

What would be worse to wear, clothes made from fish skin or shoes made of human hair?

This book will ask you to think about some record-breaking yuckiness – so make sure you have your sick bucket handy!

You know that there are world records for things like the fastest runner or the biggest ship? Well, the records in this book are a bit different. It's easy to time the speed of a runner or work out the size of a ship. But the smell that I think is the worst in the world might not be the smell that you think is the worst. So these records give you something to think about. And even better than that – they give you something to argue about!

In each group the records have sick ratings with five sick splashes being the most revolting. See if you agree, or if you think a different one is the most yucky!

Safety first

Please don't try any of the activities in this book, and don't go looking for any of the dangerous or nasty animals and plants. Don't try any of the dangerous games and please, please, please don't try to eat any of the poisons.

Chapter 1
The Nasty Natural World

There are some lovely things in nature – pretty flowers, cute kittens, fluffy chicks. But there are also some revolting and disgusting things.

Ugliest Animals

I hope that these animals have mums and dads who think they are good-looking, because I think they're not very pretty at all. Who do you think is the ugliest?

This is a lappet-faced vulture. It has no feathers on its head. Also, most of the time its head is stuck inside some dead animal that it's eating. It's hard to clean blood off you when you only have a beak, so it's always pretty grotty and scruffy all over.

The naked mole rat has no hair. Its skin is pink and wrinkly. It's a bit like a sausage with little legs and huge teeth sticking out the front!

The blobfish is a big ugly blob. Its face looks rather like an old man's face, with a big nose and mouth. It lives in the deep seas near Australia. (Check out Pic. 1 on the next page.)

Goblin sharks' skin is almost see-through. They look pink because their blood shows through their skin. They have horrid, crooked teeth, and when they want to eat something they push their teeth further out of their mouths to bite more easily! (Check out Pic. 2 on the next page.)

The fangfish looks like something from a film about aliens. It's a deep-sea fish and it's pretty scary. It's all black, has tiny little eyes and a HUGE wide mouth filled with teeth like needles. (Check out Pic. 3 below.)

Nastiest Animal Tricks

Some beasts are beastly and do very nasty things. Which of these do you think is the nastiest?

A starfish uses suckers on its feet to hold on to shellfish and then it pulls in different directions to rip the shellfish apart. The starfish then uses a nifty trick. It sends its gut out of a tiny hole in its body to go round the shellfish and eat it.

When a hagfish is scared, it turns the water around it into disgusting slime. The slime kills anything that wants to eat the hagfish. One hagfish can turn 20 litres of water to slime in a few minutes!

Do you ever get told off for being nasty to your brother or sister? Bet you're not as nasty as a shark. Some sharks eat their brothers or sisters before they are even born! That way only the strongest shark lives.

Boys, you better make sure you never go out with a spider. Many girl spiders eat their boyfriend spiders as soon as they have mated. And when their babies are born, some mum-spiders feed them on their own sick! Others lie down and let their babies kill and eat them. Once there is none of the mum-spider left, the babies start to eat each other.

A sea cucumber is a type of sea slug. If it's scared that a fish might eat it, it shoots part of its guts out through its bottom. The fish eats the guts, and the sea slug can get away. It can grow more guts and do the whole thing over again.

Nastiest Nibbling Things

A parasite is an animal or plant that lives on or in another living thing. Parasites play nasty tricks. Which do you think is the worst?

Parasite wasps lay their eggs inside maggots, which are baby flies. While the maggots grow into flies, they make themselves a hard case. The wasp eats the maggot when it's changing, so when the case opens, the wasp comes out rather than the poor fly!

One kind of parasite likes to live in herons. It gets into the heron's body by hiding inside fish which it turns orange. Herons spot the orange fish and eat them, and so the parasite gets inside the heron, where it wanted to be all along.

Young horse-hair worms live inside crickets. But when they grow up and want to find a mate, they need to live in water. So the worm gets into the cricket's head and turns it mad so that the cricket jumps into the water. The cricket drowns and the worm wriggles out.

A really nasty kind of tapeworm lives inside tadpoles. As the tadpoles grow into frogs, the tapeworm makes them grow extra arms and legs at odd angles. These monster-frogs can't hop or swim well, so they get eaten by water birds which carry the tapeworms to new ponds. There they infect new tadpoles.

Some fruit-fly maggots live in the heads of ants and eat their brains. This turns the ants into zombies. They walk around with no brain until at last their heads drop off. The maggots live in the ants' dead bodies until they turn into flies.

Nastiest Plants

It's not just animals that can be nasty to each other. Some plants play pretty nasty tricks, too. Which of these do you think is the worst?

The Western Australian Christmas tree doesn't bother getting water from the ground for itself. Its roots tap into the roots of other plants so it can steal water from them instead.

The strangler fig grows round and round another tree and chokes it. In the end, the tree inside dies and rots away. The strangler fig is left in its place.

One type of fungus grows inside insects. When it is ready to spread its seeds, it breaks out through the insect's body to the outside world. Here is an ant with the fungus growing out of its head.

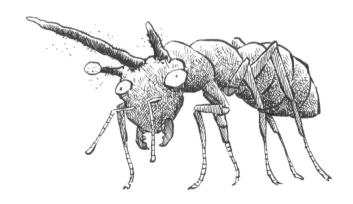

The pitcher plant is a plant that eats animals! The plant is shaped like a cup with steep, slippery sides. Small animals or insects that fall in can't get out. There's a pool of acid at the bottom which the plant uses to turn them into a tasty soup. Yum ... bug soup.

The venus fly trap is a plant that bites! It has special 'traps' that look a bit like open clam shells, with tiny prickles inside. When a fly walks across the prickles the trap closes. The plant then uses acid to turn it into a yummy fly smoothie.

Smelliest Smells

Sweaty feet? Your brother's farts?
Rotten eggs? They have nothing on these
horrible pongs! Which do you think is the
stinkiest?

Sewers – everything that is flushed down
our toilets ends up in the sewers, so you can
imagine how nice it smells down there. Yuck!

Sick – how bad your sick smells depends
on what you have eaten or drunk. It can be
very bad.

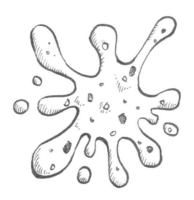

The corpse flower smells truly nasty. It is a giant lily that lives in forests in Indonesia. It only blooms every few years – and that's just as well because the flower smells like a rotting dead body.

The skunk is an animal that lives in North and South America. When it's scared it squirts a chemical from a gland near its tail. The smell of the chemical is so bad that it drives away anything that might want to attack the skunk.

In the Second World War, the French came up with a cunning plan to fight the German army. They called it 'who-me?' It was a chemical that smelled like rotting dead bodies and was supposed to be the worst smell ever. The French thought it would leave the Germans with red faces as if they had farted!

Chapter 2
Why Would You Do That?

Most Horrid Hobbies and Habits

Do you have a nasty habit or hobby? Some people pick very odd ways of passing their time. Which do you think is the worst hobby out of these?

Niek Vermeulen from the Netherlands collects sick bags from planes. He has more

than 6,000 from over 1,100 different airlines.
All empty ... I hope.

Kanchana Ketkaew from Thailand likes to
spend time with scorpions. Once she spent 33
days in a glass room measuring 12m² with
more than 5,000 scorpions. She was stung 13
times.

Christine Martin from West Sussex once
sat in a bath of maggots for one and a half
hours. Can you imagine? They would crawl
all over you! Yuck!

Wen Xide from China eats live snakes. He started in 1999 when he ate one to win a bet, and now he likes to have a beer and a live snake as a snack.

Ken Edwards from England holds the world record for eating live cockroaches. He once ate 36 in one sitting. Cockroaches carry lots of diseases, so don't try to break his record!

Extreme Experiments

At school the first rule of science is to be careful so you don't hurt yourself. Some scientists are not so careful. Which of these do you think is the worst?

An English computer expert called Kevin Warwick put microchips into his own body as part of his study of robots.

A German doctor called Werner Forssman cut a hole in his arm and pushed a tube into it. The he pushed the tube along his blood vessels all the way to his heart – then took an X-ray of himself

An Italian scientist called Lazzaro Spallanzani swallowed tiny fabric bags of food tied to strings. He waited a while, then

pulled the bags back up his throat to see how the food was being broken down in his stomach.

In the 1880s, the famous scientist Louis Pasteur wanted to help prevent a deadly disease called rabies. People can catch rabies if they are bitten by a dog that has it. Pasteur sucked spit from the mouth of a dog with rabies to use in his experiments.

An American doctor called Stubbins Ffirth wanted to know how yellow fever passes from one person to another. So in 1802 he cut open his arm and poured in the sick of a person with yellow fever. When that didn't work he dripped the sick in his eyes, swallowed some, and then drank some of the person's blood!

Super-revolting Meals

What is the worst food you have ever eaten? Lumpy custard? Sprouts? Broccoli? There are much nastier foods in the world – and some people think they are really nice! Here are my top ten most revolting foods. How would you like any of these for dinner tonight?

In Indonesia, people eat small bats. They look a bit like skeleton mice with huge mouths and lots of teeth. They are served piled up on a plate, because once you start, you can't stop!

People in Indonesia also snack on deep fried monkey toes. They just suck the toe off the bones and throw the bones away.

There is a type of bird in Indonesia that makes its nest from spit. Chefs in China make soup from the nests. They call it 'birds' **nest** soup' but it's really 'bird **spit** soup'!

In China, people stuff mouse babies or lizards into bottles of rice wine to make a tasty drink. The animals are often put in while they are still alive as this is supposed to make the flavour better.

In Cambodia people eat crispy fried spiders. They first started eating them when there was not enough food in the country. It seems they were so tasty that they're still a popular snack even though there are other things to choose now.

The Inuit people live near the North Pole where it is too cold to grow grapes to make wine. They make seagull wine instead. Seagull wine will make you really glad you're too young to drink. The recipe is easy –

STEP 1: Find a seagull and put it in a large jar. A dead seagull is good, but a live one will do if you can get it in the jar.

STEP 2: Fill the jar with sea-water.

STEP 3: Put a lid on the jar and leave it in the sun for a few months. The seagull will rot and make an alcoholic drink.

STEP 4: Enjoy!

In Sardinia, an island near Italy, people eat a cheese called 'casu marzu'. Casu marzu is not just smelly, it's crawling with live maggots. In fact, it's not just crawling with maggots – the maggots can jump up to 15 centimetres into the air! It's now against the law to eat the cheese. Sometimes the maggots can carry on living in people's guts and make them ill.

People in Thailand drink snake blood, sometimes straight from the snake. It's very expensive – which could be just the right excuse for saying you don't want any.

Balut is a popular snack in Asia and it is really, really revolting. It's a duck egg with a partly-grown baby duck inside. The egg is boiled and the baby duck is eaten whole – bones, beak and all.

Reindeer droppings are small and round like berries. Some tribes eat the droppings raw and crunchy, but others cook them in blood soup. Yum yum – reindeer poo in blood.

All in the Name of Beauty

People do some really revolting things trying to make themselves more beautiful. How far would you go to be beautiful?

There is a spa in Japan that gets people to soak in a tub of noodles and pork soup to make their skin soft. The noodles are fake, but the soup is from a noodle shop!

In Japan people also like to lie in hot, smelly, slimy mud. They use real mud from volcanoes.

Some massage shops in America use corn snakes to do all their work. The snakes wiggle over customers' backs, shoulders and even heads to give them a warm and wiggly massage. Just as well corn snakes don't bite ... very often!

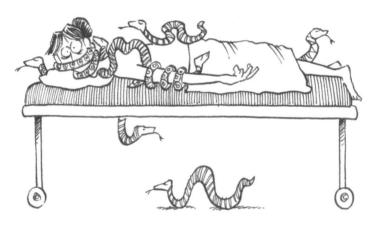

Japanese women have used special bird droppings to make their faces whiter for hundreds of years. Now a beauty salon in New York sells a face mask made from bird poo. They leave it on for 50 to 60 minutes, and it costs around $200.

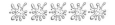

Leeches look a bit like slugs, and suck blood from people or animals. Some beauty salons offer the chance to have your blood sucked by leeches. They say it cleans your blood. (How? The leech eats it!) Some other salons put leeches on people's faces to get rid of spots. Eek! I'd rather have the spots.

Is it Art?

We've all made a mess with paint at one time or another. But imagine the mess you'd make if you painted with poo or blood. Which of these do you think is the most revolting work of art?

The artist Chris Ofili makes paintings with elephant dung. At first he used dung from Africa, but now he gets it from London Zoo. His paintings don't hang on the wall – they all stand on two legs made from dried

elephant dung. Chris dries the poo in an
airing cupboard.

The artist Marc Quinn makes a model of
his own head every five years. That doesn't
sound too bad, right? Wrong! He makes the
model by freezing his own blood. Each head
is made of four and a half litres of blood
which Quinn takes from his body slowly over
five months.

James Ford made a ball of snot called
Bogey Ball. He collected his bogeys in an egg
cup for a few years until the ball was big
enough. How big is big enough? It's 21
centimetres across.

The artist Damien Hirst cut a cow into
slices with a power saw, then put slices in
glass cases. There's space between the cases

so you can walk between them and see the insides of the cow.

Damien Hirst also made a glass box full of maggots. There is a rotting cow's head in the case for the maggots to eat. They turn into flies and then they are killed by an electric fly-killer in the top of the box.

Chapter 3
Bad Sports

Fair Play?

We all like a good game – but some games are rather nasty. Would you like a game if you were going to lose your head if you lost? Which of these games do you think is the worst?

Maggot racing is just like horse racing – only with maggots and no riders. The maggots race against each other on a striped board. Each maggot has to keep to its own strip, or track. Sometimes they have to crawl over sticks. The course is about 30 centimetres long – which is a long way for a maggot.

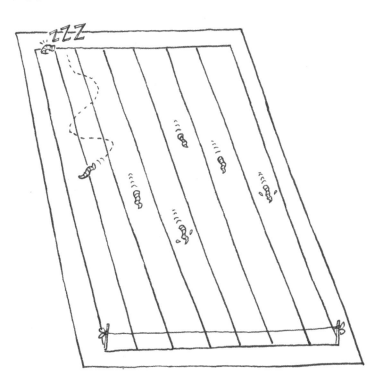

Eating competitions became popular about a hundred years ago. In a competition in 1916, four men who had just arrived in America from other countries had a bet to see who could eat the most hot dogs in a set time. Some ate till they were sick! The winner ate 13 and everyone said he was the best American. And in 1919 a man called Ping Bodie had a pasta-eating competition with an ostrich. He won – the ostrich fainted.

Hundreds of years ago in Europe, people liked to watch bear fights. They chained up the poor bear and made dogs attack it. The dogs and bear fought and often both were hurt. Bear fighting still happens in Pakistan.

Long ago the Aztecs in South America played a game rather like basketball. The players had to try to get a rubber ball through a stone hoop, but they were not allowed to touch it with their hands. Unlike basketball, the losing team were killed as human offerings to the gods. Or possibly the winning team were killed. We don't really know. Whichever way, it doesn't sound as good as a nice gold medal!

The Romans liked to watch bloody sports in round theatres. Gladiators – soldiers with swords – would fight with each other or with wild animals such as lions or bears. People were often killed in these fights. Other times, slaves or prisoners with no swords or armour had to fight gladiators or wild animals. You can guess who lost.

Bad Kings and Things

Rulers should try to protect their people. They might not always get it right, but only really bad rulers kill the people they are supposed to look after. Who do you think is the worst king out of this lot?

Ivan the Terrible ruled Russia from 1533 to 1584. He had thousands of people tortured or executed. He used to carry a stick with a spike on the end to stab people who upset him. He even killed his own son with it in an argument.

The Roman emperor Commodus ruled 1,800 years ago. He was a very bad ruler who had lots of people killed – even his sister. Commodus liked to play at being a gladiator. He fought with wild animals and other gladiators. But he wasn't brave – he cheated. The animals were tied up so they couldn't hurt him too much. Once he killed 100 bears in just one day. The other gladiators he fought only had wooden swords while he had a real one. Carved words on one statue of him say that he killed 12,000 men.

Sultan Ibrahim 'The Mad' ruled Turkey 400 years ago. He had 280 wives, who were not allowed to set eyes on any other men. It is said that Ibrahim was told that another man had been visiting his wives in secret, and he was so cross he ordered that the wives should die. Most of them were tied into sacks and drowned in the river.

Qin Shi Huang ruled China from 246 BC to 210 BC. Two wise men promised to make a spell to make him live longer, but they couldn't really do it. In revenge he had 460 wise men buried alive.

Vlad the Third ruled part of Romania 500 years ago. He was very cruel. He was called 'Vlad the Impaler' because he had his enemies impaled (or stuck) on spikes. We think Vlad killed around 100,000 people. He was also called Dracula, but he wasn't a vampire. Dracula meant 'son of the dragon' in Vlad's language.

War Games

There is a saying that all is fair in love and war. But some things are just too unfair. Which of these do you think is the most revolting trick?

A Persian man called Timur led an attack on the city of Delhi in India in 1398. The Indian army had elephants wearing armour. They made the elephants rush at their enemies. But Timur tied wood and straw on the backs of camels, and set fire to them. He made the burning camels run at the elephants. The elephants panicked and trampled on the Indian army. Timur took the city and killed the people who lived there.

Long ago, archers often dipped their arrows in dirt or blood. The wounds the arrows made became infected, so the poor soldiers they had hit were sure to die.

In 184 BC, the African leader Hannibal had his men throw clay pots filled with snakes onto the decks of his enemies' ships. The snakes bit the sailors. At different times in history other armies threw pots of scorpions or pots of plague germs.

When settlers from Europe went to live in America and Australia, some gave the native people blankets and clothes that had been used by people who had smallpox. Their plan was to make the native people die of illness so that the new settlers could take their land.

The army of Mongolia attacked the city of Caffa in a really revolting way in 1347. They used a big catapult to toss the dead bodies of people who had died of plague over the city walls. The people in the city caught plague and many died.

Look What I've Got!

Prizes and trophies are nice things to show off. I bet you'd show off a football trophy or a swimming prize. But would you have liked to show off these things?

In the old days, people often made nasty objects from dead animals. One of the worst was feet from dead elephants made into tubs to hold umbrellas and walking sticks.

Celtic warriors in Britain 2,000 years ago used to cut the heads off enemies they killed in battle. They often put them on show over gates and doors.

Some tribes in the Amazon rain forest used to cut the heads off their enemies and make them into shrunken heads. To make a shrunken head, they used to remove the skull and fat, sew the skin around a wooden ball, boil it and then use special plants to stop it rotting.

Warrior tribes around the world made drinking cups from the skulls of enemies they killed. The oldest skull cup ever found is nearly 15,000 years old.

HIC!

There is a small hill with a grim history near Kyoto railway station in Japan. It is called the Mimizuka Mound, and it was made from a huge pile of ears and noses cut off Korean soldiers the Japanese killed in battle in 1592–98. The Japanese soldiers were paid for each person they killed. So they packed the ears and noses into barrels of salt water and sent them to Japan to be counted.

Chapter 4
What a Way to Live!

Some people have really nasty ways of living – quite revolting, some of the things they do.

Clothes to Make Your Skin Crawl

You think your school uniform's bad? It could be much worse! Which of these would be the worst to wear?

How about some sandals made from human hair? 500 years ago in Korea, people made sandals from their own hair as a gift for someone they loved, or as a sign of hope that a sick person would get better.

There is nothing like a border of puffin beaks to make your apron look nice. In Alaska people wore aprons made from deer skin to take part in special ceremonies. They decorated the aprons with deer claws and puffin beaks.

People in the east of Russia used to make jackets and coats from the skin of fish. Nice and scaly. And probably quite smelly, too.

How would you like a pair of trousers made from the throats of seals? The Inuit people near the North Pole used to make clothes from the insides of animals. The throat of a seal is just the right shape for a trouser leg. Use two seals and you can make a nice pair of trousers.

When you live near the North Pole you get cold hands a lot – but that's OK, you can wear gloves. As bears don't seem to get cold, it seems like a smart move to make your gloves from bear skin. Better still, make them from hollowed-out bear paws with the claws still on!

Home-not-so-sweet-home

How would you like to live in a hole? Or on a pole? Which of these would be the worst place to live?

Around 400 AD a man called Simeon went to live on a platform on top of a small pillar in the desert to prove his faith in God. He stayed there for 39 years. The platform was only 1m², and it didn't have a toilet. It must have been a bit messy underneath!

People who live near the North Pole, where it is very cold, often live in igloos made entirely of blocks of snow. It's small, and cold and the walls are always white.

More than a thousand years ago, a few people with very strong faith in God asked to be sealed up in tiny rooms to prove it. A priest said the prayers used for a dead person being buried, then the person was sealed into the room. They never came out, and everyone in their town or village behaved as if they were dead.

Some people in Mongolia live in large tents called yurts. Yurts are made of felt, and the felt is made from old camel hair and yoghurt. I suppose you could eat it if you got really hungry!

Living in a house is nice – but perhaps not if your house is made of cow dung. In parts of India, people make houses from dried cowpats, stuck together with runny cowpats. Too much rain changes the house back to a pile of poo!

Worst Animal Homes

Things could be worse. You could be an animal that has to live somewhere really awful. Perhaps these creatures don't mind ... Which do you think is the worst?

Remember the birds' nest soup they eat in China? The male birds make a cup-shaped nest from their own spit, stuck to rock. The spit hardens, and the baby birds hatch in a solid nest of spit!

A seabird in South America called the booby makes a nest from poo. Luckily the poo is dried out, so perhaps it doesn't smell too bad for the baby boobies.

Dung beetles collect animal poo and roll it into a large ball. They lay their eggs on the ball and the baby maggots eat the poo when they hatch.

Bluebottles are fat flies with a shiny blue body. They lay their eggs in rotten meat, dead animals, rubbish, or dung. The eggs hatch into maggots that eat the nasty stuff they live on until they are ready to turn into flies.

Lots of insects, worms and other small creatures live in dead bodies. In fact, there are so many that the police can tell how long a body has been dead by the types of creatures they find in it.

Worst Work

What's the worst job you have to do? Cleaning out your hamster? Taking the rubbish out? Think yourself lucky! You could have to do one of these jobs! Which is the worst out of them?

Did you know that bird and bat poo can be worth a lot of money? It can be used to make fertiliser for plants. To sell it, people collect it in big baskets. Not a nice job, especially if you have to go into a cave of bats with droppings 1m deep on the floor!

Rich Romans liked a good feast – in fact they often liked it a bit too much. They sometimes ate and drank so much they were sick. Their poor slaves had the job of waiting at the back to clear up the vomit!

In many parts of the world, children pick over rubbish dumps looking for any items that can be sold or used. It's a smelly, dangerous job.

Do you think you would like to help hold someone down while their leg was cut off – without painkillers? In the old days, a ship's doctor had up to SIX assistants to hold down wounded sailors while he sawed off their arms or legs!

In places with no flush toilets, people can use a hole in the ground. Holes in the ground soon fill up, and so in the old days in London 'night soil' collectors went round collecting it and taking it away. Nice!

Which do you think is the most revolting record in the book?

How many sick splats would you give it?

Our books are tested
for children and young people by
children and young people.

Thanks to everyone who consulted on
a manuscript for their time and effort in
helping us to make our books better
for our readers.